Markova and Dolin in *Giselle*, Act II, 1950

ALICIA MARKOVA

by

GORDON ANTHONY

With an appreciation by
DAME ADELINE GENÉE-ISITT
D.B.E., D.Mus., M.I.etA., B.M.

PHOENIX HOUSE LIMITED
LONDON

Made 1951 in Great Britain. Printed at Plymouth by
Latimer, Trend & Co Ltd for *Phoenix House Limited*
38 William IV Street, London, W.C.2.

First published 1951

To 'Butterflies and Roses' . . .
a memory

CONTENTS

AN APPRECIATION

by Dame Adeline Genée-Isitt

D.B.E., D.Mus., M.I.etA., B.M.

To WRITE an appreciation of Alicia Markova should not be difficult, and yet I am finding it no easy task. I do not wish to be fulsome; at the same time words that sufficiently express my feelings and what I wish to indicate might very easily appear exaggerated. This is the first and obvious thing I desire to avoid.

I have followed Markova's career with much interest almost from the beginning. When she was practically at the commencement of what has become a great career, I was asked my opinion of her abilities by someone closely connected with the dancing world. My reply was: 'She will be good, for she has something to give us which, however, is not yet quite developed, especially in the placing and in the use of hands and arms.' In addition, Alicia Markova gives a lightness to her dancing that is unsurpassed.

This aerial lightness can be assisted in *à deux* and *adagio* work and Markova's partner of many years, Anton Dolin, takes full care that it is emphasized whenever possible. These two eminent artists have appeared together for many seasons and their work has become so harmonious and perfect that one feels completely at ease watching them performing the most difficult tasks.

Alicia Markova was born 1 December 1910, daughter of Arthur Tristman Marks and his wife, Eileen Mary Ruth Marks, née Barry, of Irish descent.

Mrs Marks, when her daughter had reached her eighth year, was told the child was flat-footed and knock-kneed, and the specialist suggested she should wear irons to correct certain defects and as a means of strengthening her limbs generally, adding the advice that 'some fancy dancing' might help!

At the age of ten Alicia made her first public appearance on the stage at the Kennington Theatre in *Dick Whittington*, and in 1921 she was taken by her mother to Seraphine Astafieva to begin her serious training as a ballet dancer. On 26 June 1923 Madame Astafieva organized a performance at the Albert Hall and Alicia was advertised as 'Little Alicia, the miniature Pavlova'.

Later Diaghilev noticed her when visiting the school. He was greatly impressed by her, and she was chosen to join his company in 1925. She remained a member of it until the great impresario's death in 1929. It had been his intention to revive *Giselle* and for Markova to alternate in the

7

role with Olga Spessiva. This was regrettably made impossible, but during her stay under the Diaghilev banner she had danced the title role in Stravinsky's *Le Rossignol* and the cat in *La Chatte*.

The death of Diaghilev was tragic for many artists of the day and not least for one, like Markova, just on the threshold of her career. She and others strove to keep ballet alive in England, and when the Camargo Society was formed in 1930 she was invited to create the leading role in Ninette de Valois' ballet, *Cephalus and Procris*, with the delicious music by Grétry and décor by William Chappell.

Upon the foundation of the Ballet Club, with Marie Rambert as the prime mover and Frederick Ashton as one of the heads of the organization, Alicia Markova was again invited to dance for them in *La Peri*, a ballet Ashton specially created for the opening of the club, 16 February 1931. She appeared during four years on Sunday nights for the Ballet Club and danced there for the first time in *Aurora's Wedding* and *Les Sylphides*.

The year 1932 saw a new connection. The Vic-Wells company gave matinées at the Wells and at the Old Vic evening performances. She was the leading danseuse at Sadler's Wells, from autumn 1933 until May 1935. *Giselle*, *Casse Noisette*, and *Lac des Cygnes* were revived in their entirety for her, and I think I am correct in saying she was the darling of the Wells and acclaimed by the public at all and every performance during that period.

When she danced in the full-length version of *Lac des Cygnes* on 20 November 1934 the *Daily Telegraph* wrote: 'Last night the role of the Swan Queen was danced with surpassing grace and beauty by Markova. It is to be doubted if it has ever been done more perfectly.'

Since then she has danced the part of Giselle in many countries, especially in America. In New York, at the Metropolitan Opera House, she was partnered by Serge Lifar as Albrecht, and later she and Dolin appeared there together on many occasions with the greatest success.

On their way out to America in 1939 the war changed their plans and during their prolonged stay in the U.S.A. they were instrumental in creating an interest in English dancers and dancing, generally by accepting engagements with the Ballet Theater and by touring all through the vast country. During the war travelling there, as here, was no joy and very tiring, especially when on 'one-night stands'!

Now I am happy to see Markova home, with no less artistry and great in the many exquisite roles she has added since she and Dolin formed the Markova-Dolin Ballet, touring the British Isles for two years, doing great pioneer work for English ballet.

It is therefore right and fitting that to-day Markova and Dolin are at the head of the Festival Ballet Company (a title suggested, I believe, by Alicia Markova) consisting of a British *corps de ballet*, but with many famous foreign artists invited to appear together with Markova, All have been acclaimed by the public, but none more than Markova and Dolin.

To my mind, dancing contains all that is beautiful, for the beauty of all other arts is incorporated in its science. Markova has contrived to combine so much in her dancing of these other arts, and has made one whole of it. Her musical instinct is apparent in all her parts.

Her quiet expressions, her rather wry smile, and her movements are all combined to make one harmonious whole in whatever part she undertakes.

All this is not achieved without many sacrifices, which we of the Dance know only too well. It is occasionally said that technique does not make an artist, but I contend that without it there is no lasting development in the artist as such.

I am happy to end my words by saying 'thank you' to one who has never spared herself in her duties to Terpsichore and who will go down in the annals of history of the Dance as our first great ballerina to become world famous.

AUTHOR'S PREFACE

In 1925, when on a visit to my sister Ninette de Valois in Monte Carlo, shortly after she had joined the Diaghilev ballet, I was introduced by her to a very small and alarmingly frail young girl of fourteen with a serious and pale 'El Greco' face framed by sleek black hair; I particularly remember her lustrous dark eyes. This was little Alicia Marks, known to the company as Diaghilev's latest 'idea' (in those days a child of fourteen could not be taken seriously in a company of famous and mature artists—what *could* he do with such a one?). As usual Diaghilev was right, and Stravinsky's *Le Rossignol* was specially revived with 'my little English girl' in the title role, her first leading part. Diaghilev's 'idea' came off, and that night a star was born. Her next most important role was that of the cat in *La Chatte*, shortly before Diaghilev's death in 1929. Meanwhile she had danced smaller roles, as Red Riding Hood in 'Aurora's Wedding,' from *The Sleeping Princess*, and the little American girl in *La Boutique Fantasque*, which were the first roles I saw her in.

The death of Diaghilev caused complete chaos in the world of ballet. The dancers dispersed all over the world, and Markova, like many others, was left with nowhere to go. In England the Camargo Society was formed for serious ballet, also Marie Rambert's Ballet Club (now known as the Ballet Rambert) at the tiny Mercury Theatre. After various music-hall and other engagements with Anton Dolin, Markova danced for both these organizations as ballerina, creating many leading roles in modern ballet, as well as the classics, for Marie Rambert—among them the Aurora *pas de deux*, *Les Sylphides*, *Swan Lake*, etc.

In 1931 the Vic-Wells Ballet (now the world-famous Sadler's Wells Ballet) was formed, and Markova joined it as prima ballerina in 1933. She still danced as guest artist for Marie Rambert. Ninette de Valois revived the great classical ballets in their entirety for her. Two of them, *Swan Lake* and *Casse Noisette*, had never been seen in their entirety in this country before. Markova danced her first full-length *Giselle* and *Casse Noisette* in January 1934, and *Swan Lake* in November of the same year. She also created several new roles for the company, including *The Haunted Ballroom* (April 1934) and *The Rake's Progress* (May 1935) for Ninette de Valois, and *Les Rendezvous* (December 1933) for Frederick Ashton. I always preferred her in the romantic ballets; she will ever remain a *danseuse sentimentale* to me, and as such she has been unsurpassed. In my opinion Markova will remain a legendary figure in the history of ballet, in particular for her rendering of such ballets as *Les Sylphides*, *Casse Noisette*, *Swan Lake*, and, above all, for her *Giselle*.

In 1935 Markova left the Wells and founded her own company with Anton Dolin which, after a very successful tour of the provinces, opened its first London season at the Duke of York's Theatre on 23 December 1935. They danced mainly classical roles but revived La Nijinska's *The House Party*, originally known as *Les Biches* (May 1937) and Markova danced the leading role in the revival of Nijinska's *The Beloved One*, in which she gave a performance of unsurpassable beauty.

In 1938 she joined the Ballet Russe de Monte Carlo as their leading ballerina, and in 1941 she joined Ballet Theater in New York, where she electrified American audiences with her performances of the romantic ballets, especially *Giselle*, also creating more modern roles. After this she toured America with Anton Dolin, her equally famous partner, sometimes with their own company and often as guest artists to other companies.

In 1948 Markova returned with Dolin to dance with the Sadler's Wells Ballet again, as guest artists at Covent Garden, in *Giselle, Swan Lake*, and *The Sleeping Beauty*. It was the first time she had danced the full-length version of *The Sleeping Beauty*—a further step in her great classical career, made, appropriately, with her old associates of the Wells. Here it may be interesting to quote extracts from Ninette de Valois' preface to my book *Markova* in 1935:

'Markova is of Jewish-Irish extraction, the former bestowing a foresight that amounts to second sight, whilst the latter has shown what an imaginative spirit in search of a Utopian adventure can find . . . her ethereal appearance and extreme lightness are allied to a true understanding of style, exceptional line, precision, and musicality. . . .

'Her intense surety, grace, and ease of execution may at the moment outshine her dramatic and mimetic powers. . . . Markova's rapid rise to fame during the last eighteen months demands constant achievement . . . a complete maturing and mellowing of her work must be left to the future. . . .'

After sixteen years these qualities remain, and Miss de Valois' prophesy is happily fulfilled.

Markova is now scintillating at the head of her own company—the Festival Ballet—which she founded in 1950.

BOOKS BY GORDON ANTHONY

Markova, 1935
Ballet, 1937 (with Arnold Haskell)
Vic-Wells Ballet, 1938
John Gielgud, 1938
Massine, 1939
Russian Ballet, 1939 (with Arnold Haskell)
Margot Fonteyn, 1941
The Sleeping Princess, 1942
The Sadler's Wells Ballet, 1942
Air Aces, 1944
Ballerina, 1945
Robert Helpmann, 1946
The Sadler's Wells Ballet at Covent Garden, 1947
Dancers in Colour and Monochrome, 1948
Margot Fonteyn, 1950

ACKNOWLEDGMENTS

SOME thirty-six years or so ago, as a very special treat, I was taken to the Coliseum to see Adeline Genée, one of the greatest ballerinas of her day, the toast of London and the old Empire. Little did I realize that I should one day have the honour to be indebted to her for a most gracious and charming 'appreciation' written for me on another world-famous ballerina. But it has come to pass, and my gratitude is as great as my appreciation was of her exquisite dancing —wonderful little feet that literally 'twinkled', a radiantly happy personality, perfect poise, beautiful little hands that were more eloquent than words, and a breath-taking *pizzicato*.

I also wish to thank both Madame Markova and Anton Dolin for their very kind and friendly co-operation at all times.

To Bernard Peacock I am most grateful for the use of his very excellent archives and for personal assistance.

Last, but not least, to my publishers, especially John Baker and Lona Mont-Clar, for their help and encouragement.

THE PLATES

Alicia Markova,

Dame Adeline Genée-Isitt, D.B.E.

1. Katie Willows, *The Lord of Burleigh*

Markova first created the role of Katie Willows in Frederick Ashton's *Lord of Burleigh* on 30 April 1932, at the Savoy Theatre for the Camargo Society. This picture was taken during the Sadler's Wells Ballet (then the Vic-Wells Ballet) revival on 17 October 1932. A small but enchanting role absolutely suited to her personality and exquisite lightness.

2. Portrait, *Les Rendezvous*

The first performance at Sadler's Wells on 5 December 1933 of this one-act ballet by Frederick Ashton, composed for Markova, was most exciting. Since 1929 Markova had rapidly improved technically and dramatically; she had 'grown up'. Her performance in this ballet has never been bettered. Light as air, brilliant, gracious, and scintillating—it *was* Markova.

3. *Giselle*, Act I

Apart from performances by the Camargo Society in 1932, this ballet had not been seen in England for many years, and on 1 January 1934, the Old Vic was packed for the first full-length production by an all-English cast. Markova gave a fine rendering, her solos being of exquisite ease and lightness, and her mad scene showed a strong sense of drama.

4. *Giselle*, Act II

In this act we had the Markova who was to become incomparable and world renowned.
Exquisitely floating, drifting, and gliding, she was the epitome of fantasia and the spirit
world. I was carried away by Markova's art—her musicality is of the highest grade, and
she seemed to move as part of the music like a tree in the wind.

5. The Sugar Plum Fairy, *Casse Noisette,* Act III

Casse Noisette was first seen in England in its entirety when Ninette de Valois had it specially revived for Markova by Nicnolas Sergueeff on 31 January 1934, at the Sadler's Wells Theatre. This revival, with Robert Helpmann as her partner, triumphantly added yet another great classical role to Markova's repertoire.

6. Alicia, *The Haunted Ballroom*

The first creation by Ninette de Valois for Markova when she was with the Vic-Wells Ballet; it was produced at Sadler's Wells on 3 April 1934. This ballet of ghosts was well suited to Markova, with her lightness, speed, lovely lines, and general litheness—one believed in this lovely ghost, and I have never seen this role so perfectly done since.

7. Odette, *The Swan Lake*, Act II

On 20 November 1934, at Sadler's Wells, the Vic-Wells Ballet gave the first full-length version ever seen in England of *The Swan Lake*, with Markova and Helpmann. The purity and delicacy of Markova's performances were well known, but again one remarked that strange attractive quality of hers which would seem aloofness or coldness in some dancers, but in her was neither.

8. Odette (Portrait), *The Swan Lake*, Act II

The above portrait was taken in 1934 at the same time as plates 7, 9, and 10. Many people have spoken of the great similarity between Markova and Pavlova, both in physique and as executants. It is, therefore, of interest to note that the brilliants in her head-dress pictured above were those worn by her famous predecessor.

Markova and Dolin in *The Swan Lake*, Act III, 1948

9. Odile, *The Swan Lake*, Act III

When this famous act was first seen in England Markova seemed literally possessed—all technicalities, including the *fouettés*, were attacked in a new way. Hers was a truly sinister Magician's daughter. Her smile was as bright and hard as her sequin-covered costume, her dancing was scintillating, in complete contrast with Act II.

10. Prince Siegfried and Odile, *The Swan Lake*, Act III

Markova, with Robert Helpmann, shortly before the first performance of the full-length production in 1934. She is wearing the dress, incomplete, shown in plate 9. Markova followed up her exquisite performance in Act III with a moving and dramatic fourth act which proved she had the necessary staying powers for the full-length classical ballets.

11. The Betrayed Girl, *The Rake's Progress*

The role of the Betrayed Girl, first performed on 20 May 1935, was the second created for Markova at the Wells by Ninette de Valois. Despite the general excellence of her performance I thought the quaint and stylized movements ill-suited to her; her ethereal quality and Gallic appearance seemed singularly at odds with the robustness expected of a Hogarthian character.

12. The Betrayed Girl, *The Rake's Progress*

To my mind this portrait bears out my contention that Markova appeared Gallic rather than the typical round-faced, plump Hogarthian English girl. But nothing alters the fact that she gave a fine performance, proving that her work was capable of filling a larger canvas than that of the traditional classics.

13. Nicolette, *Aucassin and Nicolette*

On 27 January 1936, Markova created the role of Nicolette in Wendy Toye's ballet *Aucassin and Nicolette*. It was a slight but charming ballet, and once again a type of role different from that usually danced by her suited her admirably. Particularly I remember a very lovely *pas de deux* with Anton Dolin, her equally famous partner.

14. The Nightingale, *The Nightingale and the Rose*

Revival created and produced by Anton Dolin, from Oscar Wilde's story, for Markova at the Duke of York's Theatre on 8 February 1936. After Markova's dancing in Stravinsky's *Le Rossignol* in 1927, this ballet must have seemed child's play, but lovely play it was. It called for all Markova's bird-like qualities, with results that delighted both laymen and balletomanes.

43

15. The Water Lily, *The Water Lily*

This was a solo arranged by Anton Dolin for Markova, to Liszt's third Consolation, on tour in November 1935. It was entirely suited to Markova's many assets. The picture shows the very lovely line of her *arabesque*, and here again is the strong resemblance to Anna Pavlova.

16. A Study, *Vanity*

The ballet *Vanity* was created for Markova and Dolin in the *Mother Goose* pantomime at the London Hippodrome in 1936. Many strict balletomanes, and I was one, deplored this appearance on the boards of music-hall, but it was good for the cause of ballet in general. Fears that the tinsel of music hall would affect Markova's work proved groundless.

The Prelude, *Les Sylphides*, Portrait, 1949

17. The Mazurka, *Les Sylphides*

This picture was taken during the first tour of the Markova-Dolin ballet in 1935, and shows her soft and easy line of *demi-arabesque*. It seemed to me that Markova had been born dancing *Sylphides*; I had seen so many of her performances in this ballet, and always I felt that it must surely be her best—there were times when she scarcely appeared to touch the ground.

18. The Woman in Blue and the Young Man, *The House Party*

Les Biches was revived by Bronislava Nijinska as *The House Party* for Markova and Dolin at the King's Theatre, Hammersmith on 3 May 1937. Dolin danced the role originally taken by Wilzak, and Markova the part created by Nemtchinova for Diaghilev. Despite the fact that the ballet now appeared dated, both Markova and Dolin gained personal triumphs.

19. The Woman in Blue, *The House Party*

In this ballet Markova proved herself fully equal to a *chic* but dated style, but I, personally, felt that she preferred to continue in her own line of classical and romantic ballets. This subsequently proved correct, showing she had the foresight mentioned in Ninette de Valois' Foreword to my first book on her in 1935.

20. The Muse and the Poet, *The Beloved One*

First created by Bronislava Nijinska in 1928, this ballet was revived by her for Markova
and Dolin at the King's Theatre, Hammersmith, on 10 May 1937. I felt that the part of
the Muse suited Markova better than all her other modern roles to date—her slim figure
in its cloud of star-spangled tulle created an illusion of almost celestial beauty.

21. The Muse, *The Beloved One*

A portrait taken of Markova as the Muse in *The Beloved One*. Something of the almost celestial beauty I referred to under plate 20 is shown here in her large expressive eyes, which struck me so forcibly at the time I first met her when she was only fourteen.

22. The Muse, *The Beloved One*

This studio picture of Markova in the role of the Muse has always been a favourite of mine, and her performance gave me much the feeling of the swirling light and stars on the background I devised for it. Fleeting white clouds, stars, and flashes of light were, for me, synonymous with Markova's dancing.

23. Odette, *The Swan Lake*, Act II

On 13 May 1937, at the King's Theatre, Hammersmith, *The Swan Lake* was given in its entirety for the first time by the Markova-Dolin Company, the second English company to do so (the Wells in 1934 was the first). Markova was the *prima ballerina* both times. To her natural style, schooling, and finish Markova had added *brio*, especially in Act III. Complete assurance now rounded her performances into a perfect whole.

24. Odette, *The Swan Lake*, Act III

Markova's physical likeness to Pavlova is particularly noticeable here, otherwise there is little in common between them. Temperamentally Markova is entirely different. Pavlova could be dynamically, almost violently, dramatic at times; she had superb lightness coupled with a vivid personality and character, but for this reason lacked Markova's impersonal aloofness. It is this difference which, for me, makes Markova unique among famous ballerinas.

25. The Bluebirds, *The Sleeping Beauty*

A study of Markova and Dolin in this most famous and much overworked *pas de deux* taken during their Coronation season at Hammersmith. Markova sparkled as few have ever done in this role—she had everything—slight figure, superb technique, lightness, speed and precision, coupled with the fine showmanship and fine partnering of Anton Dolin.

26. *Les Sylphides*

I believe this is the only photograph of Alicia Markova, Frederick Franklin, and Markova's sister, Bernice Barry, who was a promising member of the Markova-Dolin Ballet at the time of their Coronation season. It appeared in the *Bystander* in February 1938, with the news that Markova was to join the Ballets Russe de Monte Carlo, run by Leonide Massine and the late René Blum.

27. *Les Elfes*

First produced in 1924 as *Elves*, and brought to the Coliseum Theatre, London, by Fokine, on 31 May 1937, it was revived by the Ballets Russe de Monte Carlo at the Municipal Theatre, Monte Carlo (where this portrait was taken), with costumes by the late Christian Bérard. The part created by Nana Gollner in London was now shared by Markova and Mia Slawenska.

28. *Les Elfes*

The Markova-Dolin Ballet disbanded at the end of 1937, and Markova joined the Ballets Russe de Monte Carlo in Monte Carlo, where this picture was taken in April 1938. Her dancing was excitingly lovely, as with transparent wings she literally flew through the air, and dazzled one with the speed of her *pirouettes*.

29. The Gods, *The Seventh Symphony*

The Seventh Symphony was created and produced by Massine for the Ballets Russe de Monte Carlo in Monte Carlo on 5 May 1938, where this picture was taken. In the Third Movement, the brightest and loveliest, Markova and Igor Youskevitch were The Gods. Markova, perfectly cast, was described by the *Bystander* as 'exquisite in her smooth delicacy and lightness'.

30. Giselle and Albrecht, *Giselle*, Act I

On 26 July 1938, at Drury Lane, Markova and Lifar danced *Giselle* for the first time together. It was some time since I had seen Markova dance the part, and I could not wonder at her fame in the role. Her shy, girlish gaiety in the first part of this act was well balanced with her mad scene, which had new dramatic depths.

31. *Giselle*, Act II

Study of Markova in the second act of *Giselle*, taken during the 1938 summer season at Drury Lane with the Ballets Russe de Monte Carlo. In the second act she appeared to be full of a distant, dreamy, spiritual tenderness towards the dying Albrecht—her pleading with Myrtha for his life was indeed that of one spirit appealing to another for the life of a mortal.

77

32. *Giselle*, Act II

A further study of Markova in the second act of *Giselle*, as she appears before her veil is
torn aside by the Queen of the Willis to bring her to life.

79

33. *La Camargo*

Nearly every dancer at some time or another likes to have her name coupled with this famous eighteenth-century dancer, as with Taglioni or Pavlova. This study of the solo arranged by Ninette de Valois was taken before an R.A.D. Production Club performance at the Westminster Theatre on 18 July 1939.

34. *La Camargo*

A twentieth-century portrait of Markova as the famous eighteenth-century danseuse. It will be remembered that Camargo was the first celebrated danseuse to shorten her dress for dancing, thereby showing her ankles, and the temerity required to do this must seem remarkable to this generation in view of the general laxity of morals in eighteenth century France.

35. Portrait, *Le Cygne*

Fokine revived a special version for Markova of the solo created in 1905 and made famous by Anna Pavlova, who danced it for the first time in England on 18 April 1910 at the Palace Theatre, London. In January 1949 at Empress Hall, Earls Court, Makova danced it for the first time. I did not see Pavlova dance this, but I can well imagine from Markova's romantic rendering how its creator made it world-renowned.

36. *Le Cygne*

This second picture of the Dying Swan was included at the special request of Markova, and it is of interest to note that her exquisite dress was made, like all her others, by Madame Manyza, who also made all those for Anna Pavlova; a Manyza 'tu-tu' is considered synonymous with perfection.

37. *Le Cygne*

The above picture shows a striking likeness to Pavlova and gives some idea of the feeling
of this touching choreographic relic of a poetic and sentimental era. It makes one hope
that at least a semblance of its lost dignity and greatness may be regained.

38. The Princess Aurora, *The Sleeping Beauty*, Act I

I had not seen Markova since she left for the States in 1939. We had heard that she had conquered America, and of her accepted suzerainty as a classical ballerina—above all in the role of Giselle. In 1948, the news that she was returning as guest artist for the 'Old Wells' caused enormous excitement and speculation.

39. The Princess Aurora, *The Sleeping Beauty*, Act I

On 12 June 1948, Markova danced her first performance of *The Sleeping Beauty* at Covent Garden, and this picture may give some idea of her continued inimitable delicacy and lightness. She looked charmingly piquant, and her precision, dignity, and poise were undiminished. Her greatly increased showmanship, balance, and finesse made up for the slight lessening of technique—it was still the well-loved Markova.

40. Prince Florimond (Anton Dolin) and the Princess Aurora (Alicia Markova),
The Sleeping Beauty, Act II

In the Vision scene, despite a head-dress which, though beautiful, was, in my opinion,
extremely unsuited to her, Markova seemed more in her element than in the first act.
Here was all the romantic scenery and feeling one associates with Markova. Amidst a
moonlit woodland lake scene, including a faery boat with gossamer sails, Markova,
darting in and out among her coryphées, was elusive and enchanting.

41. Prince Florimond (Anton Dolin) and the Princess Aurora (Alicia Markova),
The Sleeping Beauty, Act III

This last act of *The Sleeping Beauty*, widely known as Aurora's Wedding, is the most exciting and glamorous in classical ballet, and to perform the *pas de deux* and solo is the dearest wish of all would-be ballerinas. Since lightness, poise, style, and precision are even more essential than strength, Markova could not but rise to the expected heights.

42. Odette, *The Swan Lake*, Act III

On 29 June 1948 Markova and Dolin danced *The Swan Lake* in its entirety as guest artists with the Sadler's Wells Ballet at Covent Garden—a great and exciting first night, with Markova, now a world-renowed dancer, giving for the second time a London première of this revered classic with her old associates.

43. Odile and Prince Siegfried, *The Swan Lake*, Act III

This act depends greatly upon its *tour de force* and virtuosity; very often too much stress is laid upon the latter and not enough on style and dramatization—or too much on both. However, with such artists as Markova and Dolin, one would expect a good middle course, and this they followed with their usual complete assurance and sense of theatre.

44. *Giselle*, Act I

On 2 November 1950, at the Stoll Opera House, Festival Ballet revived this ballet for Markova. Anton Dolin produced, and also danced Albrecht. Although she had recently undergone an operation, she gave a delightful performance in Act I; the lightness of her solo had lost nothing since her early performances, her mad scene was now completely matured.

45. Giselle and Albrecht, *Giselle*, Act II

In the 1950 revival Markova and Dolin gave the death scene one of the best performances I have known. Markova was incredible; her slightest movement of wrist, arm, or head, completed a perfect picture, each melting into another. Of all the dancers I have seen in this act, 'Markova the wraith' stands alone.

46. The Prelude, *Les Sylphides*

The ballet of *Les Sylphides* is the most widely known of all Fokine's ballets, and one might without exaggeration say that the ballerinas' names most associated with it are those of Karsavina and Pavlova in the past, and Markova to-day. This portrait, taken in 1949, shows the lovely poise of Markova's head and the line of her body.

47. Portrait, *Les Sylphides*

Markova, in the Prelude from *Les Sylphides*, which I saw her dance at the Stoll Opera House in her Festival Ballet season, Christmas 1950. I found myself forgetting everything and everybody except this floating vision surrounded by clouds of soft white tulle—the very spirit of all that was lovely and gracious in life.

48. The Sugar Plum Fairy, *Casse Noisette*

On 24 October 1950, at the Stoll Opera House, Festival Ballet revived the full version of *Casse Noisette*, in which Markova danced the Sugar Plum Fairy for the first time since the original English production by the 'Wells' in 1934. Apart from *Giselle* and *Sylphides*, I think that of all the classical ballets this is the most suitable to show off Markova's art to perfection, especially the solo. This picture was especially chosen by Markova as typical of the dance.